Dewayne Hotchkins

This is a glacier. It forms when snow falls faster than it melts. It turns to ice. Glaciers are like rivers of ice. They are always moving. However, they move very slowly.

Glaciers form in places where there is a lot of snow. The snow builds up and turns to ice. This happens year after year. The newer layers push down the older layers.

The ice in a glacier is very **dense**. It is packed tightly together. A glacier's ice is very heavy. The weight of the ice, along with gravity, causes the glacier to move.

As glaciers move they shape the land. They can carve **valleys**. They can change the shape of mountains, too.

Glaciers can create **kettle lakes**. These form when a piece of glacial ice breaks off. It is left behind. When the ice melts a small lake is formed.

Glaciers pick up lots of rock and soil as they move. This material gets left behind to make hills.

As glaciers move, sometimes they leave long ridges of soil and rock behind.

Right now glaciers cover one-tenth of the earth's surface. During the last ice age, they covered about a third of the planet. Glaciers hold most of the world's **freshwater** supply.

The longest glacier in the United States is in Alaska. It is more than 115 miles long. It is called the Bering Glacier.

Dense ice absorbs red and yellow light. However, dense ice reflects blue light. This is why some glaciers look blue.

Glossary

dense — Containing parts that are crowded together.

freshwater — Water that is not salty.

kettle lake — A shallow, sediment-filled body of water formed by retreating glaciers.

valley — An area of low land between mountains or hills.